Word Solvers
Making Sense of Letters and Sounds

Michèle Dufresne

Heinemann
Portsmouth, NH

Heinemann

361 Hanover Street
Portsmouth, NH 03801-3912
www.heinemann.com

Offices and agents throughout the world

The author and publisher wish to thank those who have generously given permission to
reprint borrowed material:

Excerpts from *My Puppy* by Joy Crowley. Illustrated by Rita Parkinson. Copyright © 1996.
Published by the Wright Group/McGraw-Hill, 19201 120th Avenue NE, Bothell, Washing-
ton 98011. Reprinted by permission of the publisher.
Excerpts from *Scared at Night* by Deborah Charren. Copyright © 2001. Published by Pioneer
Valley Educational Press. Reprinted by permission of the publisher.
Excerpts from *My Busy Day* by Laurel Dickey. Copyright © 2000. Published by Pioneer
Valley Educational Press. Reprinted by permission of the publisher.
Excerpts from *The Big Show* by Michèle Dufresne. Copyright © 2000. Published by Pioneer
Valley Educational Press. Reprinted by permission of the publisher.
Excerpts from *George's Story* by Michèle Dufresne. Copyright © 1991. Published by Pioneer
Valley Educational Press. Reprinted by permission of the publisher.

Library of Congress Cataloging-in-Publication Data
Dufresne, Michèle
    Word solvers : making sense of letters and sounds / Michèle Dufresne.
        p. cm.
    Includes bibliographical references (p.)
    ISBN 0-325-00456-0 (alk. paper)
    1. Reading—Phonetic method. 2. English language—Phonetics. I. Title.

LB1050.34 .D84 2002
372.46'5—dc21   2002024245

Editor: Leigh Peake
Production service: Colophon
Production coordinator: Sonja S. Chapman
Cover design: Joni Doherty
Compositor: LeGwin Associates
Manufacturing: Steve Bernier

Printed in the United States of America on acid-free paper
09   08   VP   6   7   8   9

Contents

Acknowledgments

This book would not be possible without the inspiration and support I have received from colleagues and friends. I want to thank all of the classroom teachers and Reading Recovery professionals with whom I am so fortunate to work—especially my colleagues at the Plains School in South Hadley. Special thanks to Dee McWilliams and Sandy Roth, teachers and literacy coaches who have opened up their classrooms to me, and who have generously shared their many insightful ideas. I am extremely grateful to Linda Garbus, who read and reread the manuscript, and who gave me numerous helpful suggestions. I am also grateful to my husband, Bob, who supports my many projects, and who took time to put his red pen to my rambling sentences. Finally, I would like to express my gratitude to my friend and colleague Laurel Dickey (whom my husband calls my other half); she continually challenges me to question my thinking and practice.

Introduction

When I was a junior in high school, a special education teacher asked me to tutor a fifteen-year old girl who was reading at a second-grade level. The text I chose for her to read was the driver's education manual. I knew she wanted to learn to drive. My thinking was that since she would need to read and answer a series of test questions to get her driver's permit, she would be highly motivated to read the driver's manual. Of course, there was the problem of the unknown words. I could read them easily. How come she couldn't? I went to a nearby university library and checked out some books on phonics. I found that there are many combinations of letter sounds that can be blended together to make a word. I attempted to teach her the sounds, and we struggled our way through the driver's education manual. Each day, after she worked on phonics and then attempted to read the manual, I would read to her from a novel for teens. For both of us, that was the favorite part of the session. You won't be surprised to learn that I didn't teach her to read—however, I do believe she got her driver's license.

For a long time as a classroom teacher, I continued to struggle with children who had difficulty learning to read. What kind of phonics instruction should I provide? And how should phonics instruction fit into my literacy program? Recent research confirms that knowledge of letters and their sounds is important. Phonological awareness (the awareness that there are words within sentences, syllables within words, and phonemes within syllables and words) and phonemic awareness (the awareness that words are made up of individual sounds) are strong predictors of a child's ability to learn to read (Opitz 2000; Adams 1990). Children need to have explicit instruction in phonics, and this instruction should be both powerful and meaningful (Fountas and Pinnell 1996). However, it is also important to understand that children do not need to know all their letters or sounds to begin to read (Clay 1991).

This book is designed to assist the busy teacher in implementing phonemic and phonological instruction within the framework of a well-designed literacy program. The following topics will be discussed in the book:

- *Designing authentic instructional opportunities for teaching about letters and sounds.* Letter-sound relationships should be taught explicitly and within an authentic reading or writing context. At times teachers will present lessons about letters and sounds in isolation, drawing from observations of the children's engagement with reading and writing of continuous text. The teacher's focus will always be directed toward supporting the children's understanding of how to use their new learning while reading and writing.

- *Building instruction on children's strengths and needs.* Letters and sounds need not be presented in a predetermined order. Although some published programs for teaching phonics promote the idea that teachers should teach letters and sounds in a certain sequence, there is no ideal scope and sequence for teaching children about letters and sounds. It is far more powerful to tailor instruction to take advantage of children's strengths and to address their specific needs. This requires that teachers not only be knowledgeable about how to provide instruction, but also be skilled at observing students.

- *Helping children develop an extensive core of words they can easily read and write.* Beginning readers can use the words they know to check that their reading is correct. As readers increase the number of words they know, they do not need to problem solve each word as they read. Good readers read smoothly and accurately because they control a large number of words they recognize very quickly.

- *Teaching children to recognize spelling patterns in unknown words.* Letter-by-letter sound analysis of unknown words is much more difficult than looking for distinguishing features of groups of letters or known parts of words. Letter-by-letter analysis is usually less reliable and more time-consuming. The brain quickly integrates visual information from two known parts of a word—much more quickly than sounding out single letters.

- *Promoting flexible problem solving of new words.* Proficient readers will actively work to solve an unknown word (Clay 1991). When one way of solving a word doesn't work, they try another. Using visual information (e.g., how the letters look) is just one strategy for solving new words.

- *Supporting instruction with manipulatives.* There are many opportunities for teachers to teach about letters and sounds throughout the day. Using manipulatives to support this teaching can be very powerful. (Nevertheless, it is important to emphasize that manipulatives are not meant to supplant reading and writing activities, but rather to be used as a tool to support children learning to work with print.) In particular, magnetic letters have many useful applications. For example, they can be used to help children learn about the small visual differences between different letters, or about the ways some words can look alike, or about how to break apart words to reveal known parts, or about how to make new words from known words.

Chapter 1 contains a brief summary of the reading and writing process and the literacy events that support a comprehensive literacy program. Chapter 2 explores letter learning and how teachers can support children to learn to look at print. Chapter 3 examines the importance of helping children gain a useful set of core words that they can write quickly and can easily recognize in print. Chapter 3 also furnishes teachers with strategies for helping children gain skills at learning new words. Chapter 4 analyzes how known words can be used to problem solve new words, and contains suggestions on supporting children as they learn to problem solve new words. Chapter 5 discusses ideas for organizing a classroom to support instruction about letters and words.

Chapter 1

Learning to Read and Write

Before considering how to provide phonics instruction, it is necessary to understand how the reading/writing process works. Phonics instruction that a teacher provides will always be for the purpose of helping children become better readers and writers—not merely good phonics doers!

A second-grade teacher once confessed to me that she had decided it was "magic" that made the children learn to read. It is definitely amazing how children learn to read. Sometimes it does seem magical. But no matter how simple it seems to be for some children to learn to read and write, literacy learning is very complex.

Marie Clay (1991) defines reading as "a message-getting, problem-solving activity, which increases in power and flexibility the more it is practiced" (6). Good readers use several sources of information to make meaning from text. Readers use the background knowledge they bring to the text and the meaning they are constructing as they read to help them anticipate what is coming next and confirm that what they are reading makes sense. Readers also use language structure to support their reading. Readers can check how the reading sounds against what they know about how language works (*Does what I am reading sound like language?*). The language structure also provides readers with anticipation for what is coming next and powers the reading forward (*What language do I anticipate next*?). In addition to meaning and structural information, readers use the visual information from print—both the orthographic (how words look) and the phonemic (how letters sound)—to anticipate what is coming next and to confirm that what they are reading is correct. Good readers use all these sources of information in a highly skilled and effortless manner. When a skilled reader is reading, an observer may notice brief hesitations, but mostly the reading is smooth as the sources of information come together into phrased and fluent-sounding reading.

Good literacy teaching focuses on supporting children to use all the sources of information available to them in their reading. Teachers need to encourage children to use their oral language and their knowledge about the world. But above all else, teachers need to remind children that their reading should always make sense.

All readers need to be able to look at print and use it efficiently and effectively so that they can solve problems quickly, all the while keeping meaning and structure in mind. A friend describes this as a juggling act. All the balls are in the air. Your attention may be drawn more to the ball coming down, but you must keep the other balls in mind.

The focus of this book is on teaching children how to look at the print and problem solve unknown words. To explore the teaching of early literacy in greater detail, I highly recommend *Guided Reading: Good First Teaching* by Irene Fountas and Gay Su Pinnell (1996), and *Apprenticeship in Literacy* by Linda Dorn, Cathy French, and Tammy Jones (1998).

Start with Assessment

Skillful teaching begins with careful assessment. It is essential that teachers observe children to gather information to help in deciding what to teach next. Some of this observation can be informal, but at times it will be necessary to gather more formal observations.

Informal Observation

Informal, ongoing literacy assessment can be interwoven throughout the day and doesn't need to be cumbersome. This might mean carrying a clipboard with Post-it notes or stickers for jotting down observations. (See Figure 1–1.) Later these observations can be transferred to a notebook with a page for each child. Information such as how the child is responding to the teaching, what confusions the

Figure 1–1   Teacher taking informal notes on a child's reading

child exhibits, and what understanding the child demonstrates can provide valuable information for making teaching decisions. When observing beginning readers working with text, a teacher will want to note specific behaviors:

- Whether the children are able to match their fingers up to text
- Whether the children are making up words using the picture, but not attending to the words or letters in the book
- Whether the children are controlling directionality, such as left to right and return sweep
- Whether the children can find and point to known words in the text

As children begin to work with more complex text, a teacher will want to note how the children approach problems in the text. Are they stopping and asking for help? Are they rereading and searching the picture for clues? Are they sounding out unknown words letter by letter, or are they breaking the words into known parts?

Systematic Observation

Informal observations alone can be misleading. At times, a teacher needs to take stock with a formal literacy assessment. Marie Clay created *An Observation Survey of Early Literacy Achievement* (1993a) for just such a purpose. (How to administer the Observation Survey will not be discussed here.) It is strongly recommended that teachers use the Observation Survey as an integral part of assessing a students' literacy progress. The Observation Survey is used to gather information on children's letter knowledge, their ability to hear and record sounds in words, their ability to recognize and identify a core of high-frequency words, and their understanding of concepts of print. As part of the survey, teachers observe children's language and record children's language structure and the level of control they have with it. (Another tool for observing children's control over oral language is the *Record of Oral Language and Biks and Gutches*, Clay et al. 1993.)

Part of Clay's Observation Survey is the *running record*. Running records are a tool for recording and analyzing children's reading behaviors. Running records can provide a teacher with information to determine the appropriate text level for a child, to monitor the rate of a child's progress over time, to assess a child's overall literacy progress, and to make grouping decisions. Teachers will find using the running record of text reading a powerful tool for recording a child's reading behaviors.

Text used for running records can come from a variety of sources. Teachers can learn a lot from taking a running record on a text the child has read once before. For example, on Monday Lin was introduced to, and read, I *Can Read* with her guided reading group. On Tuesday her teacher pulled Lin aside for five minutes and took a running record while Lin read I *Can Read* for a second time. The assessment allowed the teacher to examine Lin's reading behaviors with a book that was somewhat familiar and to gather information about the appropriateness of the book for Lin.

Here are some important reading strategies the teacher might observe:

- Does the reader notice and attempt to correct errors? Or does the reader keep reading even when the reading doesn't make sense, sound right, or look right?
- Does the reader attempt to read in a phrased and fluent manner? Or is the reading slow and word-by-word?
- Does the reader use the punctuation? Or is the reader reading through the punctuation?

- Does the reader attempt to problem solve new words? Or does the reader stop and appeal at difficulty?

Here are some reading behaviors the teacher might observe when the reader encounters an unknown word:

- Does the reader stop and do nothing?
- Does the reader ask the teacher for help without first trying something independently?
- Does the reader sound out the word letter-by-letter?
- Does the reader use known words to solve the unknown word?
- Does the reader look for known parts in the unknown word?
- Does the reader reread the text searching for more information?
- Does the reader study the picture?
- Does the reader try something else when one thing doesn't work?

Running records that are taken with text previously used during guided reading give teachers direct information on the appropriateness of the text for each child and on the reading behaviors children are using following instruction. The second reading should fall somewhere in the instructional range (90 to 94 percent accuracy) or the easy range (95 to 100 percent accuracy). It is critical that the text not be too hard. When text is too hard, children begin to struggle and use less appropriate strategies. They learn much more from reading text that is instructional or easy. *Running Records for Classroom Teachers* by Marie Clay (2000) is an excellent resource for teachers who wish to learn more about using running records in their classrooms.

Running records can be taken on unseen text. Some school districts, in an effort to gather information about the reading progress of their early primary students, have begun to use a selection of leveled text as periodic benchmarks of a student's reading progress. *The Developmental Reading Assessment* (Beaver et al. 1997) is an example of a group of published texts for this purpose. The teacher is provided with a short introduction to give the child before each reading. The child reads the text, or a portion of the text, and the reading is recorded with a running record. (See Figure 1–2.) Following the reading, the child is asked to retell the story, and may be

Figure 1–2   Teacher taking a running record

asked some comprehension questions. This assessment provides the teacher and the school system with an overview of the progress of individual children. The information gathered from the running record, as well as the retelling, can be very useful for making teaching decisions. An alternative to the use of published texts for assessment is possible. The school district can simply set aside a collection of leveled books to be used for assessment purposes. A team of teachers may wish to create book introductions for each book to standardize the assessment procedure.

Literacy Events to Support Beginning Readers and Writers

Reading Aloud

Many children come to school with limited storybook reading experience. It is imperative for teachers to allow plenty of time for reading aloud to children. The stories can and should be read over and over again, giving children multiple opportunities to hear interesting, rich language with varied vocabulary. Later, these opportunities to hear complicated language structures and rich vocabulary will support children when they come across the language structures and new and varied vocabulary in their reading (Clay 1991).

Shared Reading

During shared reading the teacher and children read together in unison. This can be accomplished with an enlarged text, such as a big book, chart, or text on an overhead. Alternatively, the teacher and children may each have a small book. Shared reading can be done with the whole class or a small group. When the teacher and children reread a shared text, it provides children with opportunities to notice and use information they may have missed the first time. Shared reading can provide a great opportunity for word study. Children can find and point out useful sight vocabulary, identify letters, and look for words that look and sound alike. To read more about shared reading, I recommend *Perspectives on Shared Reading: Planning and Practice* by Bobbie Fisher and Emily Fisher Medvic (2000).

Guided Reading

Guided reading provides an opportunity for the teacher to work with a small group of children. The group members will almost always be at the same reading level, because the text the teacher uses with a guided reading group needs to be carefully selected to match the students' instructional level.

During guided reading the teacher introduces the book to the children. In the introduction the teacher gives information about important ideas in the book, discusses the overall plot of the story, and uses, in certain situations, some of the new language structure children will encounter. At first, this can feel strange to a teacher, almost as if one is "giving the story away." But the purpose here is to ensure a successful first reading of the story. Following the introduction, *all* of the children read the entire book. For the earliest readers, the first reading might be structured similar to shared reading without the teacher's voice. The children will listen to each other and try to read together. Over time, with teacher prompting, they will begin to use softer voices. With everyone reading the story, it is impossible to monitor each student's reading. This can feel uncomfortable to the teacher. Most teachers like to check on each reader to be certain everything is going well. It is more important, however, that all the children read all of the text. In the old model of round-robin reading, many children only had a chance to read a paragraph or a page of a book.

As the children read, the teacher circulates and listens to individual children. The teacher prompts the children at difficulty and praises useful strategies. The teacher must sometimes move on from someone who is struggling in order to get around and hear other children. This is a good time to take notes on what the children are doing, how they are attempting to solve problems, and where they are having difficulties.

Following the reading the teacher and children discuss the story. Then the teacher takes the children to places in the text that were difficult and does some further teaching. Chapters 2, 3, and 4 will explore ways to teach children to use visual information. For more information about selecting books for guided reading and how to implement a guided reading program, see *Guided Reading: Good First Teaching* by Irene Fountas and Gay Su Pinnell (1996).

Partner Reading

All children should have their own small box of books that they can read with a high degree of independence. Often these books are books that have been introduced and read during guided reading. During partner reading, children sit with a partner. The children sit side by side, shoulder to shoulder—and take turns reading books from their book box. This reading time helps children build fluency. For example, Joey is an early emergent reader. He reads the book *My Puppy*, a book he was introduced to the day before in a guided reading lesson. Next his partner Jamie, a developing reader, reads *The Big Snow*.

Independent Reading

This is a time for children to select and read whatever they choose. They may chose to read a big book that the teacher has read with the class many times, a chart on the wall, a book from their book box, or a book from the classroom library. Teachers can use this time to pull children aside to take running records.

Shared Writing

During this time the teacher acts as a scribe for the children, recording the group's ideas. These pieces of writing can be put up on the wall and used for rereading during a time for reading around the room. The writing is most often related to a group experience. For example, after a class trip to the pond to observe water life, the class

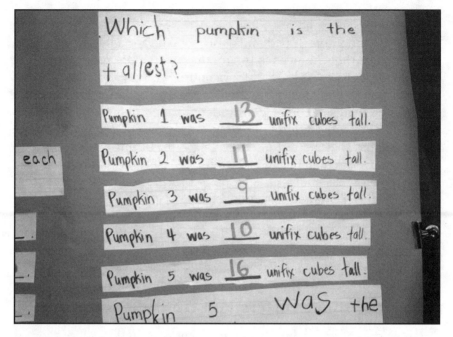

Figure 1–3   Interactive writing

might compose a recounting of the experience. Shared writing can be used to record information from a content area or to record a story a group of children has generated.

Interactive Writing

During interactive writing, the teacher and the children share a pen. Through a lively discussion, the story is jointly composed. It may be a retelling of a favorite story, a recounting of a field trip, or information about a science or social studies subject (Figure 1–3). It is important that the children who are participating have a common set of experiences on which to draw. Children, with the teacher's guidance, take turns doing the scribing. At times, the teacher may stop and do some teaching, such as demonstrating how to form a particular letter or showing how a word looks in complete detail.

For more on interactive writing, see *Interactive Writing: How Language and Literacy Come Together, K–2* by McCarrier, Pinnell, and Fountas (2000).

Writing Workshop

During writing workshop the teacher starts with a minilesson (for no more than five to eight minutes). The minilesson will focus on the craft of writing (e.g., how children can get a writing idea, make a strong ending, or add interesting details), or on management (e.g., how children can use the resources in the room to help them spell). Additionally, it may focus on skills (e.g., how children can say a word slowly and record sounds). Following the minilesson, the children write and the teacher circulates to confer with students about their writing (typically a period of twenty to thirty minutes). At the end of the workshop the class gathers together for a response group. During response group (lasting no more than five to eight minutes), several children will read a work in progress and ask the group to provide feedback. The teacher may record the children's questions on Post-its and give them to the writer to use the next day to support further writing of the piece. Response group is also used to read and celebrate completed pieces. There are many books written about writing workshop. My favorite is still *The Art of Teaching Writing* by Lucy Calkins (1986).

Learning About Letters and Words

There is no way around it. You need to know something about letters and words to read and write. However, it is clear that children can get started with very little knowledge, and through lots of reading and writing, they will learn about letters, words, and sounds. It is important that children have many experiences exploring letters and words so they learn how to look at letters and words and learn how words work (Pinnell and Fountas 1998). Teachers need to build into their daily instruction many opportunities for teaching children about letters and words. The remaining chapters will explore how manipulatives such as magnetic letters or tiles can be used to greatly support this teaching. A comprehensive literacy program must provide opportunities for children to gain skills at using the visual aspects of print to ensure children's success working with continuous text.

Teachers need to design deliberate instructional opportunities for teaching about letters and sounds. Letter-sound relationships should be taught explicitly but within the context of authentic literacy events. At times teachers will present lessons about letters and sounds in isolation, drawing from observations of the children's engagement with reading and writing of continuous text. The focus of these lessons will *always* be on supporting the children in using their new understanding to read and write continuous text.

Chapter 2

Learning About Letters

Learning about letters plays a critical role in a child's literacy progress (Adams 1990). As children learn letters, they learn to distinguish how one letter differs from another. They learn the names of the letters, and they learn the sounds associated with them. Although, as teachers, we often focus our attention on children learning letter-sound associations, it is first necessary for children to learn to see each letter symbol as something distinct from other letter symbols (Clay 1991). Learning to distinguish one letter from another similar-looking letter provides a challenge to the novice reader, especially when the letters are embedded in words (Lyons 1999). Learning to quickly distinguish one letter from another when they are embedded in a word will help children build a strong reading processing system.

Prior to entering school, most children have experiences with objects that remain the same no matter the orientation. For example, no matter how you hold a book, it is a book. When you set it flat on a table, it is a book. When you hold the book upright, it is still a book. Yet this is not so for letters. The orientation of the letter plays a crucial role! The smallest detail changed on a letter also changes the letter. The book remains a book, whether it is thick or thin, a rectangle or a square. Small loops and curves, taller stems, and extra humps can change a letter into a different letter. This of course can create lots of confusions for the novice reader and writer.

Assessing Students' Knowledge of Letters

Several tasks in Clay's *An Observational Survey of Early Literacy Achievement* (1993a) provide very useful information about individual children's understanding of letters. In Clay's Letter Identification Task the children are each shown fifty-four letterforms. The fifty-four letters include uppercase, lowercase, and the typeset *a* and *g*. The children are asked to identify them any way they can: by letter name, by letter sound, or by a word that begins with the letter. In about two or three minutes with each child, a teacher will have a clear idea of the children's ability to identify letters.

In another useful assessment task, the Dictation Task in the *Observational Survey*, the teacher dictates a sentence to a child and asks the child to say the words slowly and record the sounds. The task enables teachers to determine whether the child can hear and record a letter associated with a particular sound. Teachers may find that some children respond by drawing pictures instead of letters. Some children will make letter-like forms or tell the teacher they know what letter it is but don't know how to make it. These children may have had very few opportunities to learn about letters or to learn how to discriminate sounds and associate letters with sounds.

In a third observational task, Clay's Concepts About Print, the teacher can determine whether children understand the difference between a word and letter, whether they can find a lowercase letter to match an uppercase letter, and whether they can find the first and last letter in a word. The three Observational Survey tasks provide teachers with useful information to help in planning letter-learning activities for their children.

Getting Started

For children who have very little knowledge of letters, their own name is probably a good place to start. McCarrier and Patacca (1999) find that "powerful networks of learning can be built around children's own names" (45). Young children have a personal connection with their names. For example, my friend's four-year-old son, Zachary, notices the *z* in *pizza* and wonders what his name is doing on the pizza box! He feels personally connected to the *z* and is now learning that the *z* isn't just for his name but can be used in other ways to make different words. This linking from what is known to something new provides a more meaningful learning experience, especially for the child who knows very little about print.

Magnetic letters are a great resource for teaching children about the letters in their names and more about letters in general. The tactile, kinesthetic elements of handling the magnetic letters can be very helpful to children. The opportunity to touch and manipulate the letters provides a motor connection and supports children's ability to remember (Clay 1993b).

Here are some things to try with magnetic letters and the child's name:

- Place magnetic letters needed to make a child's name into a sealable plastic baggie, along with a card with the name printed on it. Have the child use the magnetic letters to make the name on the card under the printed name (Figure 2–1).

- Place the child's name in uppercase letters in one sealable plastic baggie and lowercase letters in another. Have the child match the upper- and lowercase letters.

- Have a group of children make their names with magnetic letters. Then have them find letters their names have in common.

- Have children make each other's names with magnetic letters. Place a photograph of each child in the sealable plastic baggie along with the magnetic letters and the printed name card.

Figure 2–1   Child making his name

There are many different ways a teacher can help call the children's attention to their name. Labels over the coat rack and on the children's desks or tables are very effective. So are cards with printed names for tracing or copying. During interactive writing, charts with chants containing the children's names and name charts that support hearing sounds in words make powerful instructional tools for literacy learning. See Pinnell and Fountas's book *Word Matters: Teaching Phonics and Spelling in the Reading/Writing Classroom* (1998) for more on using a name chart.

Using Magnetic Letters to Teach Visual Discrimination

Magnetic letters allow children to look more closely at letters. The following are some activities that can be done with magnetic letters:

- Examine distinctive visual features of letters, such as the parts of a letter that are straight or round.
- Look for the parts of a letter that make it different from another similar-looking letter.
- Recognize the same letter in different forms, such as upper case and lowercase or the typeset *a* and *g*.
- Build speed at recognizing a letter when embedded in an array of other letters.
- Quickly recognize letters that commonly are confusing to children, such as *b* and *d* and *h* and *n*.

The following activities require a large magnetic easel. Use them with a group of children who have similar letter knowledge.

- Have the children take turns to sort the letters in their names from an array of other letters. Start with letters that look very different from the letters in their names, so as not to confuse the children. After they find the letters, have them make their name. Once the children can do this quickly, have them find the letters in their name from an array of letters that look similar to the letters in their names.
- Place an array of letters that are both tall and short on the magnetic board. Ask the children to separate the letters that are tall from the letters that are short.

- Place letters that are round (*o*, *a*, *d*) and letters that are straight (*l*, *f*, *t*) on the board. Have students separate letters that are round from letters that are straight. Discuss letters that have both features.

- Have children find letters they know from an array of letters placed closely together on the board. Start with letters they know well.

- From an array of letters, have children find all of one particular letter.

- Have children find and match uppercase and lowercase letters. This is a more advanced task and should be done only after they can easily recognize the lowercase letters.

It is easier for children to find the new letter if the other letters on the board are known letters to them or if they look very different from the new letter. In the beginning, use letters that are distinct. (See Figure 2–2.)

Some examples of easier sorting tasks:

- Sort *t* from *m*, *o*, and *q*
- Sort *c* from *w*, *j*, and *l*
- Sort *y* from *n*, *e*, and *h*

Later, have children sort from letters that are similar. It is a more difficult task to find a new letter from an array of letters that are similar in shape and size.

Some examples of more complex sorting tasks:

- Sort *h* from *n*, *u*, and *m*
- Sort *a* from *e*, *d*, and *c*
- Sort *b* from *d*, *q*, and *p*

Early on you may want to have the letters spread apart on the easel. Keep in mind, however, that children need to discriminate letters imbedded in words (Clay 1991). As students become more proficient at finding the letters, place the letters closer together. Look for the speed of recognition to increase.

According to Clay (1991), children beginning to discriminate between letters are developing more than one system for identifying or distinguishing letters—for example, phonemic, alphabetic, and visual. Although naming letters is a way of identifying letters, it is not

Figure 2–2   Children sorting letters

the most important understanding of letters. Some children have a difficult time calling up the name of a letter. Nevertheless, many can look for, and find, letters when asked. For the children who have a difficult time remembering the names of letters, ask them to find a letter that *you* name. When they find it, ask them to say the letter name.

There are many different ways to approach letter sorting. Some children will not be able to find a letter that the teacher names. Others will be able to find a letter, but they will not be able to name it. Here are four different ways a teacher might ask for the letter *r* after placing fifteen letters on the board (Figure 2–3).

1. The teacher pulls out an *r*. "Here is an *r*. Can you find some more *r*'s?"

2. "Can you find the *r*, like the *r* in *rabbit* on our alphabet chart?"

3. "Can you find the *r*, like the *r* in Erica's name on the classroom name chart?"

4. "Can you find the *r* like the one in the word *run* that we know?"

In these four examples, the children do not need to call up the name of the letter *r*.

Later, when children know all the letter names, the teacher can use a different approach:

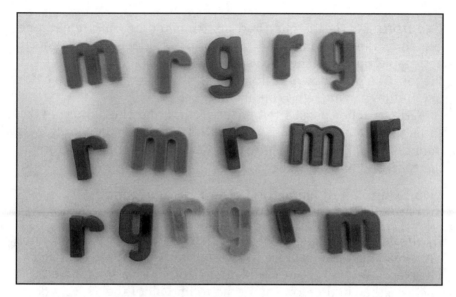

Figure 2–3   Sorting the letter r

Teacher: Find a letter you know.

Child: Here is an *r*.

Teacher: Good. It is an *r*. Find *all* the *r*'s.

Sample Lessons

Two Examples of Magnetic Letter Lessons Done in a Kindergarten Classroom

Example 1   The teacher gathers together three children who have very limited letter knowledge. She places an array of letters on the board that includes all the letters of their three names. She makes the first child's name with magnetic letters.

"That's my name!" says Ryan.

"Yes!" says the teacher. "Can you find all the letters in your name and make it say Ryan right under where I made *Ryan*?"

After Ryan makes his name and checks it against the teacher's version, the teacher replaces the letters for *Ryan* in the array and has the second child make her name.

After each child makes her name, the teacher replaces the letters, so the array of letters stays large.

Example 2   The teacher had just finished an early emergent guided reading lesson with a group of five students. Using a magnetic tabletop easel, she shows them a group of letters clustered at the top. She pulls down a *c* from the array, and says, "This is a *c* like in Courtney's name. Who can find another *c*?"

The teacher passes the easel around and the children take turns pulling *c*'s from the group of letters. This takes only one minute. They are invited to take time during choice time to return to the easel and find all of the *c*'s.

Two Examples of Magnetic Letter Lessons Done in a First-Grade Classroom.

Example 1   The teacher has grouped together six children who, while reading, often confuse words starting with the letters *d* and *b*. She places several *d*'s among an array of other very different letters. She asks the children one at a time to find all of the *d*'s. She does this again and again for several days.

After the children have spent several days practicing sorting the *d*'s, the teacher places some *b*'s in the array. Again she ask the children to find just the *d*'s. The teacher does this until the children easily find the *d*'s and pass over the *b*'s without hesitation. Then she begins to have the children find the *b*'s.

Later, when separately sorting the *d*'s and *b*'s becomes quick and easy, the teacher might ask the students to sort the *b*'s and *d*'s into two groups during the same lesson (Figure 2–4).

Example 2   The teacher has noticed that several children are stopping at known words when the words start with a capital letter. On the magnetic board he places several upper- and lowercase *i*'s, *a*'s, *g*'s, *t*'s, and *h*'s. He has each child match the uppercase letter with the lowercase letter. Then the teacher makes the word *go*. He asks the children to make the word *go* with an uppercase G. "Is it the same word?" he asks.

The children agree it is the same word; it just looks different. They talk about how it looks different. He repeats this with the words, *is, it, and, here,* and *they.*

Opportunities for Independent Practice

Name Puzzle
Place the magnetic letters needed to make a child's name into an envelope. Write the child's name on the outside of the envelope.

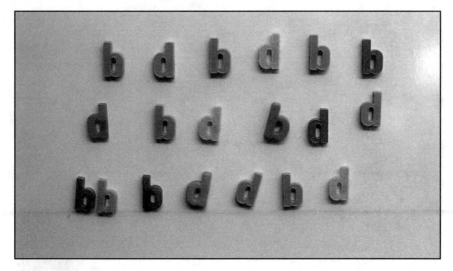

Figure 2–4   Sorting b's and d's

Have the child make, and then scramble and then make again, the name on a magnetic board. Then have the child write the name on a recording sheet. An alternative to using magnetic letters would be to make the child's name on heavy paper. Cut the name up and place the letters in an envelope with the child's name on the outside of the envelope.

Letter Name Search
Create a letter search containing letters from the names of many different children. Have the children find and circle the letters in their name—or highlight the letters with a highlighting marker.

Muffin Cup Letter Sort
Place several copies of three different magnetic letters into a container. Label the cups of a muffin container with different letters. Have the children sort the letters into the correct cups. (Instead of muffin cups you can use other small containers, such as plastic yogurt containers.) Have the children record the number of each of the different letters found.

Animal Sort
Place many copies of three different letters in an array on a large magnetic board. Have the children sort the letters. Make three large pictures for use in sorting the letters. For example, you could make

Figure 2–5   Child searching for letters

a big cat for the children to sort the *c*'s, a turtle for sorting the *t*'s, and a bear for sorting the *b*'s.

Letter Search

Have children look for words around the classroom starting with particular letters. After they find the word starting with the letter, have them write the word on a recording sheet. (See Figure 2–5.)

Summary

The fluency, speed, and ease with which children can name and recognize letters are important for facilitating the building of a reading and writing processing system (Lyons 1999). It is important for children to know many things about letters, such as the letterform, the letter sound, and words that begin with the letter. Teachers can provide many opportunities for learning about letters through a variety of reading and writing experiences and through use of magnetic letters for additional practice. It is not enough to be able to recognize and name a letter—the speed of recognition is essential.

Chapter 3

Learning Words

Children learn about words from each reading and writing experience (Pinnell and Fountas 1999). As the child orally produces a sequence of words that fits the words in the text, this experience "consolidates the ways of working that were used to get the message, and allows familiar words to become recognized rapidly" (Clay 2001, 104).

The more words children know, the easier it is for them to learn additional words. This is because with a core of known words, children are able to read more rapidly, and as a result, are able to read greater quantities of text. "As children go beyond the early stages of learning to read, we would expect an acceleration in their word learning because they have learned ways of learning words" (Pinnell 2000, 25). Research has shown that rapid, automatic word recognition is related, to competent, fluent reading with understanding (Pinnell 2000).

It is clear that the more experiences children have reading, the more opportunities there will be for increasing their reading vocabulary. The beginning readers know only a few words. Perhaps they can recognize their name because of the first letter (but will be confused when they see other words beginning with that same letter!). They may recognize some other familiar words, like *mom* and *dad*. It is important to take stock of what they do know and move out from there. Clay tells us, "Teacher assumptions about what is simple can actually threaten success. First work out what the child can already do" (2001, 19). Use what the child knows to introduce the new. For example, the teacher could make the words *my* and *mom* with magnetic letters, saying, "Look at this word, *my*. It starts like the word m*om*, which you know. Listen to how they sound alike at the beginning: *mom*, *my*."

Assessing Students' Knowledge of Word

Several tasks in Clay's *An Observational Survey of Early Literacy Achievement* (1993a) provide very useful information about a child's understanding of words. In the Word Test (the Ohio version) the child is asked to look at a list of twenty high-frequency words. The teacher can note the words the child reads quickly, the words the child confuses with other words, and the way the child attempts any unknown words. In the Writing Vocabulary task, the child is asked to write as many words as possible in ten minutes. If the child cannot think of any words, the teacher will prompt the child: "Can you write your name? How about the words *mom* or *dad*? Can you write any of your friends' names, or your brother or sister's names? Can you write any little words like *is* or *it*? The teacher can determine what words the child knows how to write in complete detail, and what words the child can almost spell.

Taking a running record on a simple book with patterned text will also help teachers to determine whether children understand word boundaries, and whether they are recognizing and using words in the text. For example, using the book M*om* (Rigby Starters One), the teacher might introduce the book by saying, "This is a story of all the things Mom is doing. See here, Mom is cooking, and on this page Mom is reading." The teacher takes a running record as the child reads the book and points a finger at the words. If the child is able to point to the correct words and carry the pattern of the story, the teacher might want to try another book, giving less of an introduction. A simple, patterned book with common sight words will work best.

Getting Started

How can a teacher provide enough reading opportunities to help extend children's meager knowledge of words? Having numerous opportunities to encounter the same words while reading different books will help children increase their reading and writing vocabulary. As children read a word correctly there will be a redundancy in the text to confirm for the children that they are right (i.e., *yes, it makes sense; yes, it sounds right; and yes, it looks like that word* I *know*).

Introducing the children to little storybooks with a simple line of text and a picture to support the text is a good way to begin. Children do not need to know much about letters or words to begin reading these little books. The teacher can introduce the children to the language pattern in the book and encourage the students to use a pointing finger to match words up to the text.

When selecting these books, try to pick books with high-frequency words. (See Figure 3–1 for a list of high-frequency words.) Make sure students will see the same high-frequency words in future new books and during other literacy events throughout the day. When children are first learning how to learn words, it may take many opportunities for them to see, read, and write a word before they know it well enough to recognize it in a variety of situations.

I don't recommend using books with just one or two word labels, such as a text that reads, "A ball. A bat. A doll. A bike."

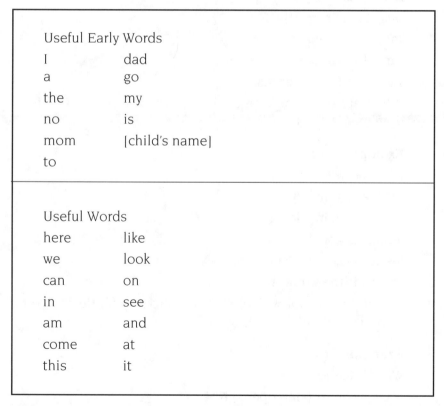

Useful Early Words

I	dad
a	go
the	my
no	is
mom	[child's name]
to	

Useful Words

here	like
we	look
can	on
in	see
am	and
come	at
this	it

Figure 3–1   Useful high-frequency words

Although at first glance they seem to be the easiest to read, it is actually easier for a child to read and remember something that is a complete sentence, such as "Here is a ball. Here is a bat. Here is a doll." It also provides more opportunities for learning words.

For a child experiencing a great deal of difficulty getting started with print, books the teacher makes with the child's name can be very supportive, because it is very helpful for the child to see his or her name. Many stories can be easily written with the child's name. These books can be illustrated with simple pictures the child or teacher draws, stickers, or even with old workbook pictures cut out and pasted in the book. These books do not need to be fancy or time-consuming. See Figure 3–2 for an example of a simple book using the child's name. Here are some more examples:

Example: Story 1

Tania Likes Fruit

Tania likes bananas.

Tania likes apples

Tania likes strawberries.

(Illustrate the book with stickers of food or pictures of food from magazines.)

Example: Story 2

Jessica's Race

Jessica is going up

Jessica is going down.

Jessica is going up.

Jessica is going down.

Jessica is the winner!

(Illustrate the book with drawings or stickers of little cars going up and down hills.)

Example: Story 3

Where Is Corey?

Is Corey here? (Flap opens) No!

Figure 3–2   Justin's book

I can go
to my friend's house.

Figure 3–3   A Busy Day

Is Corey here? (Flap opens) No!

etc.

Is Corey here? (Flap opens, with a picture of Corey) Yes!

At the same time, note that a steady diet of patterned text, while providing multiple opportunities for seeing the same words over and over again, may give children a false sense of what is involved in reading. Patterned text does not provide children the opportunity to "discover" the necessity to look at the text. (I have had children say, "I can read this book with my eyes shut!") A patterned book is only useful for helping the child understand about word boundaries (i.e., word-space-word) and how a picture can help the reader anticipate what the text says. These reading behaviors can usually be established very

I can go
to the bus stop.

quickly. If the children match their voice to the print with the aid of their finger, give them text that has a slight but supported pattern change. In Figure 3–3 from *My Busy Day* by Laurel Dickey, notice how the text changes just a little bit. The child must notice that sometimes there is the word *the*, and sometimes there is the word *my*. The language structure also supports the change, helping the child anticipate whether the word *the* will be there or not.

See Appendix D for a suggested list of books. The first set contains books that are highly patterned but contain a large core of high-frequency words. The second set of books has very small, supported changes in pattern for beginning readers. The third set, while still appropriate for the beginning reader, provides even more changes, all supported by a strong storyline and pictures.

Teachers can also make little books with a child's name to support small changes in patterned text.

Example: Story 1 with pattern changes

Tania Likes Fruit

Tania likes bananas.

Mom likes apples.

Mom likes peaches.

Tania likes strawberries.

(Illustrate the book with stickers or magazine pictures of the different fruits. Do not illustrate with the different people!)

Example: Story 2 with pattern changes (see Figure 3–4)

Jessica's Race

Jessica is going up.

Dad is going up.

Dad is going down.

Jessica is going down.

(Illustrate the book with drawings or stickers of little cars going up and down hills.)

These small changes in pattern help children learn to notice changes and then check on how well their reading is going (i.e., *yes, it makes sense, but it also looks the way I expect it to look*). Children quickly learn that they need to look at the print and check whether it has their name, or something else. This need to look at the print supports each child's learning of new words. For example, as Tania reads the little fruit book, she first knows that a page with something different from her name says *Mom*, because the teacher told her it says *Mom*. But she starts to know the word *Mom*, and she recognizes it in other places after reading her little book several times.

Using Magnetic Letters to Teach Words

Recent studies indicate that when words are looked at in isolation, children may learn words faster (Pinnell 2000). Teachers can use magnetic letters to help facilitate the learning of new reading and writing vocabulary. The teacher can give Jessica the magnetic letters

Figurre 3–4   Jessica's book

for *dad* and have her make it and scramble it and make it again several times. Jessica can use the model in the book to help remember how it looks, including the order of the letters. She can also trace the magnetic letters and the letters in the book. This tactile experience helps children remember.

Using Word Cards

Teachers can use word cards to help reinforce words the children are seeing in text. To start, the teacher might write in clear block letters several words children are trying to learn. It is good to have very familiar words along with some words that are only partially known. For children having lots of difficulty learning words, the teacher may want to type up the words in a large clear font (the size a child might see in an early reading book) so that the words look very much like the words in books. The teacher should be careful not to use print that has serifs—the words should look like the words in print.

Try to avoid having children read the words incorrectly. This increases confusion around the new word. Here is a sequence of steps to help avoid words being read incorrectly:

Step 1. The teacher places the cards out in front of the children, saying each word as it is placed.

Step 2.—The teacher asks one child to find each word one by one: "Can you find the word *go*? Find *mom*. Find *dad*." The child hands each word to the teacher. If the child picks up the wrong word, the teacher tells the child the word on the card and asks the child to trace the letters on the card and say the word. The word is returned to the array and asked for again. When children are having difficulty learning a word, ask them to trace the word and make it with magnetic letters. This will help in the learning of the word.

Step 3.—The teacher puts the words out again, saying, "Can you find a word you know?" Each child reads a word, picks it up, and hands it to the teacher.

With children who are just learning words, I recommend starting with no more than five or six words. Include the child's name and easy words, like I, so the child experiences some immediate success.

It is important to note that teaching words with either word cards or magnetic letters should not precede the reading or writing of the words in text, but should happen in conjunction with real reading and writing. Children can and do read storybooks without knowing many words or letters. Children will learn new words by reading and writing.

Integrating Word Learning into Literacy Events

Within the literacy events that happen throughout the day, teachers can make opportunities for reinforcing students' learning of vocabulary. Here are some examples:

- After a shared reading of a nursery rhyme, the teacher asks a student to come up to the chart and locate a word. After the child points to the word, the teacher places highlighting tape over the word.
- Following a guided reading lesson, the teacher does a quick check of reading vocabulary by asking the students to find and point to a few words. The words the teacher asks for are high-frequency words.
- During interactive writing, as one child is writing a word on the chart, the teacher asks another to locate the word on the word wall. Or the teacher might ask the children to all write the word on their individual whiteboard or on the rug with their fingers.
- During writing workshop the teacher notices a word a child can almost spell. The teacher shows the child the standard spelling for the word and has the child practice writing it several times on a scrap of paper.

Teaching High-Frequency Words in the Context of Reading and Writing

What follows are some sample lessons in which teachers are working to teach high-frequency words during guided reading and interactive writing lessons.

Example Lesson 1
Max, the teacher, gathers together five first graders for a guided reading lesson. All of the children in the group are able to match their figures up to the text but have a limited number of words they recognize in print. The children often make up text as they read. Max selects the book My Puppy (Figure 3–5). It has *with* only three words in it, but the text will require the children to look carefully at the print.

Introduction

Max: This is a story about a family arguing over a puppy. Here on the first page the girl says, "My puppy." But on the next page the boy says, "No! My puppy." Look, here is the word *no*. Can someone find *no* on this page?

Julia: I see it! [She points to the word *no*.]

Max: Good. That word says *no*. Can someone else find *no* on this page? [A student finds it.]

Max: Now look at the end.

Gary: It's the mommy dog. She says it's her puppy!

Max: That's right! The mommy dog says, "No! My puppy." Everyone say that with me.

Everyone: No! My puppy!

The First Reading

While the children read the book for the first time, Max circulates and praises good reading work.

Max: Jacky, I like how you are making sure your finger matches up with the words.

Max: Show me the word *no*, Nancy. Good. You found it. Make sure that when you are reading and saying the word *no*, you see the word *no*!

Following the Reading

Max asks, "What do you think? Who does that puppy belong to?"

After a brief discussion of the story, Max pulls out the magnetic letters for the word *no*.

On a tabletop magnetic board he makes the word *no* with a capital N. Then he makes it with a lowercase *n*.

Max: Are they both the same word?

Children: Yes!

Max: You are right. Sometimes the word *no* will look like this, with an uppercase N, like in your book. But then sometimes you might see it with a lowercase *n*. [Max hands several children the magnetic letters for *no*.] Make the word *no* on the table. Good. Now pass it to the person next to you so they can make it. Now let's open our books and find the word *no* again.

Once children begin building a system for learning words, teachers will find the accumulation of a reading vocabulary almost effortless. Nevertheless, at times, the teacher may wish to place some emphasis on the new vocabulary.

Example Lesson 2

Kathy, the teacher, has just finished reading a small chapter book, *Scared at Night*, with a group of first graders (Figure 3–6). She says, "Open your books to page 13. Now find the word *should* and point to it. (She places the magnetic letters out on the tabletop board.) Who wants to make the word *should*?"

Example Lesson 3

A group of kindergarten students is gathered together with their teacher, Nancy, for interactive writing. Following a field trip to the zoo they decide to start a story about their trip. They want to start with the sentence "We went to the zoo." When they get to the word *to*, Nancy asks Jennifer to come up and write the word *to* on the chart. She has observed that Jennifer knows how to spell the word *to*.

Nancy: While Jennifer writes the word *to* on the board, let's practice that word. It is a good word for you to know how to write. [Nancy writes *to* on a whiteboard slowly.] Here is the word *to*. Let's all make the word *to* on the carpet. [She erases the whiteboard and makes the word again while the children trace the letters on the carpet.] What did we all write?

Children: *to*!

Nancy: Yes. And let's look where Jennifer wrote the word *to* in our story.

Jennifer: Here it is. [She points to the word *to*.]

Nancy: You know, I think it would be good to add the word *to* to our word wall. [She writes the word *to* on a card.] Who can tell me where we should put the word *to*?

Sean: Under *Tony*'s name and the word *the*!

Nancy: Yes, Sean. You're right. *To* starts with a *t* just like *Tony* and the word *the*. [She puts the word up on the word wall.] Now let's make the word *to* a few more times so

"My puppy."

Figure 3–5   My Puppy

"No! My puppy."

Chapter 2

Camping In

Kai was sleeping over
at his friend Jake's house.
They were going to sleep
in a tent in the backyard.

"I'm tired," said Jake.
"Let's set up the tent."

Figure 3–6 Scared at Night

"O.K." said Kai.

"Where should we put it?"

"Let's put it by the shed," said Jake.

The boys got ready for bed.

They put their sleeping bags in the tent.

we can remember it when we need it. Let's make it in the air. Now let's make it on the carpet.

Opportunities for Independent Practice

Matching Game
Make up pairs of cards with vocabulary. On one card of each pair begin the word with an uppercase letter. On the other card begin with a lowercase letter. Show the children how to play the game *Concentration* with the cards.

Making Words
Give the children a few cards with words that you are helping them learn, along with a box of magnetic letters. Have the children make each word with magnetic letters, using the card as a model. The words should be ones they almost know. You can make this activity easier by putting the magnetic letters needed to make the word and the word card together in a baggie.

Rainbow Words
Place a card with a word you want the children to learn to spell. Have them trace the word with different-colored markers. Have them read the word each time they trace it.

Highlighting Charts
Give the children highlighting tape. Have them look for a particular high-frequency word and cover it with the highlighting tape (Figure 3–7).

Large-Group Activities

Making Books
Give each child a stapled booklet with the title I *Like to Eat* on the front and several blank pages inside. On the board, write in large clear letters, I *like*.

Have the children draw and color a picture of something they like to eat (stickers or magazine cutouts could also be used) on a blank page. Then have the children copy I *like* from the board and use invented spelling to write the word for the food they have drawn. Encourage the children to leave spaces between their words and to say the words slowly while they are trying to write them. When the students finish the book, write the standard spelling above the invented

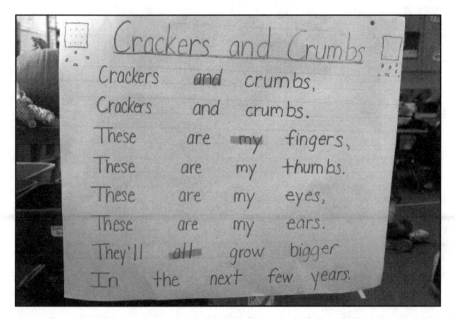

Figure 3–7   Chart with highlighting tape

spelling. This is important because the children can now use their little book to read to others. It is a bad idea to have children reading invented spelling, which could contribute to increased confusion. You always want them to have accurate text for rereading. See an example of a book in Figure 3–8. The writing over and over again of the words I and *like* reinforces the child's learning of these high-frequency words.

Here are examples of other little books children can make:

Name Books

- Jason likes (red). Jason likes (blue). Etc.
- Jason is (running). Jason is (reading). Etc.
- Jason can (jump rope). Jason can (sing). Etc.

More General Books

- I am (reading). I am (jumping). Etc.
- I go to the (library). I go to the (store). Etc.
- Here is my (mom). Here is my (dad). Etc. Here is me.

Figure 3–8 "I like" book

Finding Words on the Word Wall

Take a few minutes each day to have children locate words on the word wall. You can give clues, such as, "Who can find the word *went*? It starts with a *w* like in *Walter*."

Summary

Clay (2001) says, "Words gather information around them. Like tiny drops of mercury coming together to form drops, or raindrops running down the windowpane, words gather up information" (23). She tells us that a particular word accumulates oral language knowledge, writing and reading knowledge, quantitative knowledge about approximate frequency, personal and cultural knowledge, and spelling knowledge about likeness and differences.

Known words can be a foothold into print. But for some children, learning and remembering words will take much repetition. Teachers can provide a variety of experiences with words that will help children remember them. These words become footholds and they will go a long way to helping children in both their reading and their writing. As children develop systems for remembering words, less effort will be needed in learning new words. The first few words may take many experiences. As children learn how to remember their sight vocabulary, learning new words will occur more rapidly.

Chapter 4

Problem Solving New Words

Novice readers will encounter new words. Readers on their way to becoming proficient readers are developing a repertoire of ways to problem solve new words (Clay 1991).

Readers will use the meaning of the story, their understanding of how language works, and orthographic information to problem solve unknown words. "The text carries redundant information, more than the reader usually needs to attend to" (Clay 1991). The reader generally uses just some of the available information. When dissonance occurs (i.e., when the reading no longer is making sense, sounding right, and/or looking right), the reader must take action to search for more information—the reader needs to problem solve.

Here is an example of a child stopping to problem solve. The page contains some text and an illustration of a mouse running out into a flower garden. The text reads, "The mouse ran into the garden." The child says, "The mouse ran into the yard." Then the child stops at the word *garden*, realizing it cannot be the word *yard*; *yard* does not look right to the child. At this point the child may try to think of other meaningful possibilities (such as *flowers* or *grass*) but does not think of *garden*. To solve for this unknown word, the child will need to problem solve using some visual information (phonemic or graphophonemic information).

Word solving letter-by-letter is a very slow process that leads to many errors (Clay 1991). The brain naturally searches for larger known parts and looks for patterns in words. Research has shown that many readers use analogy to read an unknown word (Adams 1990). For example, consider the word, *quiss*. This is a word you probably can read, although likely you have never seen it in print before now. Some readers may solve the unknown word by doing a letter-by-letter sound analysis of the word. But it is much more likely that you quickly read the word without much thought. This is because you know words that start like *quiss* (*quiet*, *quickly*, etc.), and words that end like *quiss* (*kiss*, *miss*, etc.). You used the known onset (beginning - *qu*) and the rime (ending - *iss*) to construct the new word "on-the-run."

Many novice readers learn to use analogy or large word parts "on-the-run" to solve new words and do so without any direct teaching. As they build a larger and larger sight vocabulary, their ability to solve new words increases. Some novice readers need to be taught to use analogy as a problem-solving strategy. Use of magnetic letters can be an excellent starting point for teaching novice readers how to do this.

Getting Started

Choose two words that end the same way. These words need to be words the students know (for example *look* and *book*). It is important to realize that you cannot effectively teach children to go from known words to new words until they have a repertoire of words they know how to read or write.

Build the two known words with magnetic letters one above the other.

look

book

Ask the students to show you what part of these two words is the same and what part is different. Have them break the words apart.

l ook

b ook

Put out the letters to make a new word that ends the same way (Figure 4–1).

o   h   k   o

Figure 4–1 Making new words from the known word look

Then ask the students to make the new word underneath the other two words. Read the words and talk about how they almost sound and look the same.

A Sample Lesson

Mary, a first-grade teacher, has a small group of students reading at the early emergent level. They have just finished a guided reading lesson. Mary has planned a minilesson with magnetic letters that she believes will help the students in their future reading. The lesson is not something directly out of the book they have just read, but rather something appropriate to their needs. The students control most of the consonant letter sounds and have a small repertoire of words they can read. On a tabletop magnetic board, she puts up two words she knows the children can read: the word *dad* above the word *had*.

Mary: Let's read these words.

Students: *dad, had*!

Vincent: They rhyme!

Mary: Yes, they do. Good noticing, Vincent. And did you notice that something looks the same in both of these words?

Rita: They have the same letters at the end.

Mary: Yes. Please move the letters and show us where they are the same. [Rita shifts the letters at the end of each word.]

Rita: They both have *a* and *d* at the end.

Mary: Yes, they do. [She puts the words back together.] Now we are going to make another word that almost sounds and looks like the words *dad* and *had*. [She puts the letters *s*, *a*, and *d* on the board.] Who can make the word *sad*?

Brieanne: I can do it! [Brieanne moves the letters *s*, *a*, and *d* together. Mary moves the word so it is under the other two words.]

Mary: See, all three words look alike. Lots of words look and sound the same. Let's read all three words.
           Now let's try some more. Here is another word you know. [She makes the word *look*.]

Children: *look*!

Mary: Yes, now look at this word. [She makes the word *book*, underneath *look*.]

Once students understand how words can look similar, the teacher can make a word and change the first letter to make a new word. This should not be done too early, however, because seeing both the known word and the new word together helps children see the relationship. It is helpful to use two or three different examples during a lesson. These lessons are not about teaching word families or about all the words in a particular word family. The goal is for novice readers, when trying to problem solve a new word, to think to themselves, "Do I know a word like that?"

It is important to each lesson that teachers start with words the students can read. A teacher can test out a word by writing it on a whiteboard or chalkboard. If the children quickly and easily recognize the word, it can be used to demonstrate how to get to a similar new word. A reader cannot use an unknown word to link to a new word! For the lesson to be successful, students must have a core of useful words they know.

Assessing Students' Problem-Solving Strategies

Are your students able to take some action when confronting a difficulty, or do they rely on you to tell them the word? When they do attempt to problem solve, what do they do? Are they on their way to becoming independent readers? It is important to gather data to answer these questions.

Take a running record of a child's first or second reading of a text. Look specifically for the child's actions taken at difficulty to understand better whether the child is developing independent problem-solving strategies.

Figure 4–2a shows a running record taken from Jack's reading of *George's Story*. A running record is a tool for coding, scoring, and analyzing a student's independent reading of a text. See Marie Clay's book *Running Records for Classroom Teachers* (2000) for a complete description. Each check mark indicates that the child correctly read the word. The child's errors are recorded above the correct word. The arrows and the R indicate the child's repetitions of the text and the A above a word means the child appealed for help. In Figure 4–2b, Jack reads accurately and in a fairly phrased manner until he reaches the word *still*. His error, *working*, makes sense, but Jack notices that it doesn't look right. He then takes action to find other possibilities. He makes the first sound of the word and then he rereads, searching for more meaning and language information to help think what else it could be. After doing this he still doesn't know what the word is and he appeals to the teacher for help.

Jack already has several very good reading behaviors. He is self-monitoring for visual mismatches. (He notices it cannot be the word

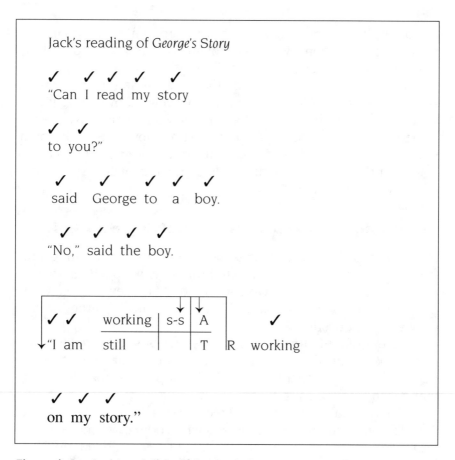

Figure 4–2a Jack's reading of George's Story

working because the word doesn't start with *w*; it starts with *s*.) He is using some visual information to problem solve. (He makes the *s* sound several times.) He is also rereading to search for more information. The teacher should praise Jack for his good work (trying to independently problem solve). But now Jack needs to learn how to use more of the visual information to solve the problem.

Learning to Use Analogy to Read and Write New Words

To begin the following instructional lessons, the students must control a sizable core of words both in reading and writing. (I recommend

"Can I read my story
to you?"
said George to a boy.

"No," said the boy.
"I am still working
on my story."

Figure 4–2b

that they know fifteen to twenty words before you begin.) The teacher
can begin to use these known words in minilessons to show children
how knowing a word can help them read and write new words. A good
time to do a minilesson is after a guided reading lesson—when the
children who are gathered together control similar sight vocabulary.

Recommended Steps: From Simple to More Complex

Step 1. Provide all the letters of both the known and the new
words.

(known words)	*can*	*day*	*got*
(new words)	*man*	*way*	*not*
(new words)	*fan*	*may*	*pot*

It is useful to prompt students for how to *use* a known word, how to
read a new word, and how to *write* a new word.
    Example prompts:

- "Here is a word you all know." (Children read the word *can*.)
- "What letters would we need to write the word *man*? It is going
  to look a lot like *can*. (The teacher puts up all the letters to make
  the word, *man*. One of the students makes the word *man*.)
- "Yes, here is the new word, *man*. What parts look the same?"
- "Here is a new word that looks like *can* and it also sounds a
  lot like *can*. How would we read this new word?" (The teacher
  makes the word *fan* under *can* and *man*; see Figure 4–3.)

The teacher repeats the procedure with the words *day* and *got*.

Step 2. Make a known word and ask the students what letter they
would need to make a new word.
    Sample teaching sequence:

Teacher: What's this word?

Students: *day*!

Teacher: What if we wanted to write a new word? What new
           letter do we need at the beginning to make the new
           word *way*?

Students: *w*. [The teacher moves away the *d* and makes the new
           word *way*.]

Figure 4–3 Making new words from the known word can

Teacher: What is the new word?

Students: *way*.

Teacher: Yes. [She then removes the *w* and returns the *d*.] Who wants to make the new word *way*? [A student removes the *d* and replaces it with a *w*.]

Teacher: Now let's make the old word *day* again. [The student returns the letter *d*. Then the teacher makes the word *may*.]

Teacher: Now what if we saw this word in a book. It looks like *day*. How would we read it?

Students: *may*!

Teacher: Yes! Which parts look the same as *day*? [A student moves the letters to show the *ay*.]

The teacher follows the same sequence with two other examples. Rather than make a lot of words that end the same (*look, book, hook, took*), it is better to use the same key word again and again over

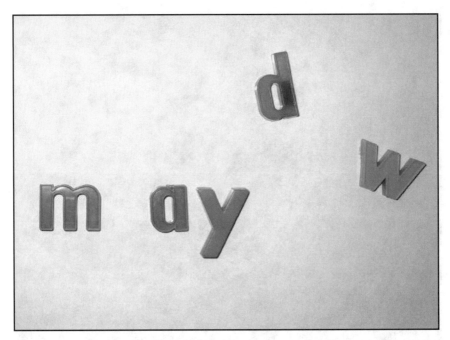

Figure 4–4 Making new words from the known word day

many lessons. Early on, it is also useful to use key words that have many words with similar endings. That way, students will begin to see the new words in text and be able to use their new skill to problem solve.

Step 3. Make the known word and put up a few letters to use in changing the first letter. Ask students to make new words and read them.
Sample teaching sequence:

Teacher: Here's a word you know.

Students: *look*!

Teacher: Who can change the first letter of *look* to make a new word? [She puts up the letters *a*, *b*, *t*, and *h*. The students change the first letters and read the new words.]

Students: *look—book*! *look—hook*!

Step 4. Prompt the students to make new words with letter clusters and blends (e.g., *day—gray*; *look—shook*). (See Figure 4–5.)

Figure 4–5 Making new and more complex words from the known word day

These teaching sequences are demonstrations for children. The teacher is showing students how they can use a word they know to problem solve a new word. The lessons should be quick—no more than three or four minutes. While the lesson can be done at a large easel with a large group, it is important that the words being used are known words. Since in a typical classroom, students' sight vocabulary will vary considerably, it is a good idea to do the lessons with small groups of students who are able to read similar texts.

Sample Lessons

Here are some sample lessons. Appendix A provides guidance on selecting words to use in your own lessons.

Day 1

1. Place the word *got* on the board. Say, "Here is a word you know. What is it?"
   (Note: If they can't read the word, it will not be useful. The words that you start with *must* be known.)

2. Make the word *hot* underneath *got*. Ask, "How are these two words alike? How are they different?" Read the two words. Talk about how the two words almost look and sound alike. Have students move the letters to show the parts that are the same. Put up the letters *l*, *o*, and *t* randomly on the board. Now ask a volunteer to make a third word, *lot*. Talk about how you can read new words and write new words using words you know. Repeat with the words *will*, *fill*, *mill*, and then repeat with the words *dad*, *had*, *sad*.

Day 2

Repeat the demonstration of the previous day using the following sets of words:

(known words)	got	will	dad
(new words)	pot	Bill	mad
(new words)	dot	hill	bad

Day 3

Repeat the demonstrations of the previous two days. Use new examples, but continue to use the same known words as well. Early on, it is best to use the same words over and over again.

Later

If students seem to have a strong grasp of how a known word looks like other words, change the known word by adding two letters to the beginning. Be sure to be clear with the children what you are doing. (For example, you could say, "Now watch how I can take away one letter and put two letters in front to make a new word.") It will be easier for the children to see the relationship of the new word to the known word if you have the complete known word on the board and you use a new set of letters to make the new word underneath.

(known words)	got	will	dad
(new words)	spot	grill	glad

Transferring into Reading

Being able to make a new word and read it with magnetic letters is not the purpose of the previous lessons. The goal is to help children successfully problem solve unknown words in text. After the teacher has demonstrated how to go from a known word to a new word, it is time to start linking the skill to the reading process.

Appendix F contains a list of prompts to support problem solving with visual information. The following examples illustrate how to use prompts to support a child who needs to problem solve a new word.

Example 1: Most Support

Billy stops on the word *stay*.

Billy: I don't know that word. [The teacher covers up the letters *st*, leaving the letters *ay* visible in the book.]

Teacher: Do you know a word like that? [Pause] *Day*. [Pause] This word is *stay*.

The teacher is prompting Billy to notice how this new word looks like a word he knows. She covers up the new part, leaving the known part exposed so that Billy can see more clearly the visual similarity. She then—after first pausing to see if he will independently make the link—tells him what word will be helpful to consider.

Example 2: Less Support

Jenny stops on the word *took*.

Teacher: Do you know a word like that?

Jenny: No.

Teacher: Cover up the beginning of the word and see if the end looks like a word you know.

Jenny: It looks like *look*! Oh . . . *took*!

When the teacher asks, "Do you know a word like that?" she is actually asking Jenny to ask that of herself. The teacher directs Jenny to cover part of the word and find something she knows. Jenny will learn from these specific directions how to do this by herself next time.

Example 3: Minimal Support

Roberto stops on the word *still*.

Teacher: What could you try?
or
What are you going to do to help yourself?

This is a much more general call for action by the teacher. Roberto should then ask himself, "Do I know a word like that?" If he needs more help to see if it is like another word he knows, he may cover up part of the word.

Transferring into Writing

Students should also use this strategy when trying to write a new word. When they are attempting to write a new word that is similar to a word they know, show them how the two words are spelled the same. This can be demonstrated during writing workshop minilessons and during interactive writing.

Example 1: Most Support

Billy is trying to write the word *had*.

Teacher: You know a word that sounds and looks like that word. [The teacher pauses to see if the child generates a word. When he doesn't, she continues to support him.] *Dad*. [She writes the word *dad* and under it the word *had* to show Billy the relationship.]

The teacher is prompting Billy to notice how this new word looks like a word he knows how to write.

Example 2: Less Support

Jenny is trying to write the word *plan*.

Teacher: Do you know a word like that? Can you find a word on our word wall that sounds like the word *plan*?

Jenny: *Can*?

Teacher: Yes, *plan* and *can* sound alike. Write the word *can* on this scrap paper. What would you change to make it say *plan*?

When the teacher asks, "Do you know a word like that?" she is actually asking Jenny to ask that of herself. The teacher directs Jenny to the word wall where she will find a word like *plan*. Jenny will learn from these specific directions how to do this by herself next time.

Example 3: Minimal Support

Roberto is trying to write the word *glad*.

Teacher: What could help you write *glad*?

This is a much more general call for action by the teacher.

Roberto should then ask himself, "Do I know a word like *glad*?" He may look up at the word wall, or simply think of words that rhyme with the word *glad*, and come up with something like *dad*, a word he knows how to spell.

Taking Words Apart

While many words can be solved by analogy, students will also need to deal with words that have multiple syllables. For example, consider the nonsense word *chinner*. In order to read this word you may have done a letter-by-letter sound analysis, or you might have thought of the word *winner*, but more likely you quickly broke the word into known parts: ch-in-n-er or chin-(n)er. The brain naturally seeks to break words between letters you do not expect to go together. Here are some examples:

stapber	stap ber	**not**	stapb er
frakhine	frak hine	**not**	frakh ine
chiptonbric	chip ton bric	**not**	chipto nbric

Magnetic letters can be used to teach children how to add parts to words or how to break words apart.

Recommended Steps—from Simple to More Complex

Step 1. Add inflectional endings to known words (*look -ing*, *play -s*). Add the ending and ask the students to read the new word. Then ask the students to add the endings and read the new words. (See Figure 4–6.)

Step 2. Place a known word with an inflectional ending on the board. Demonstrate where to break the word. Then ask the children to break off inflectional endings (*play -ing*).

Step 3. Place a known word on the board, such as *it*. Add a letter (*s*) to the beginning and have the students read the new word (*sit*). Use two or three different examples (*it - sit, at - rat, am - Sam*). (See Figure 4–7.) Move on only when the children can do this easily.

Step 4. Add letter clusters and blends to known words. It is easier to use the same cluster or blend with each example (*at - chat, in - chin*) before using different clusters and blends (*am - clam, in - grin*)

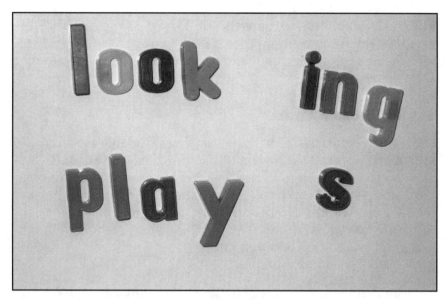

Figure 4–6 Making new words by adding inflectional endings

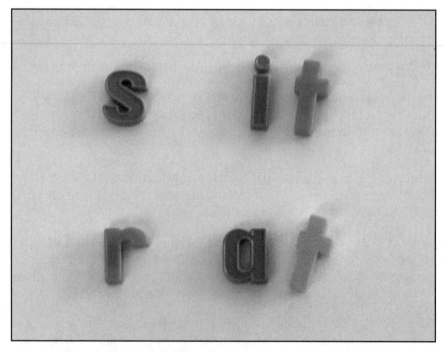

Figure 4–7 Adding a letter to a known word to make a new word

Step 5. Put up a small *known* word with a known part. Show the students how the word can be broken apart into a smaller know part (*cat - c-at*). Slide the letter *c* to the left and then read the little word, *at*. Then slide the letter back and read the new word, *cat*. Put up another, similar word and ask the students where to break the word (*s-at, r-at*).

Step 6. Put up an unknown word with a known part. Have the students slide the word apart and read the known part and then make the new word and read it (*f-all*).

Step 7. Make slightly larger and more complex words by using letter clusters or chunks that the students know (*ch-at*).

Step 8. Have students break off the end of words (*for-t, car-t*).

Step 9. Make large words that require several breaks. For words in which a consonant is doubled (e.g., *winner*), show the students how the extra letter does not change it (*w - in - n - er*). (See Figure 4–8.) It is easier to use words that are all similar (*dinner, winner, thinner*) and more challenging to use three completely different words (*chatter, sitting, slammed*). See Appendix B for suggested words.

To help students, suggest that they look for an ending and move that off first. The novice reader quickly learns how to use *ing, s, ed,* and even *er*.

Figure 4–8 Taking a new word apart into known parts

Magnetic letters are the most concrete way a teacher can demonstrate how to use analogy or break words apart. The teacher can also use a whiteboard, a small chalkboard, or even a piece of paper to show the same thing. However, it seems that the physical manipulation of the letters helps many children understand how words can be taken apart.

Teachers may find they can do these lessons with a large group, but it is most useful to have students actually move letters in order to search for known parts themselves. The larger the group, the less opportunity each student has to break words apart. When choosing words for both analogy work and breaking words apart, consider the students' oral vocabulary. If the word they are solving is not a word they know and use in their oral vocabulary, it will be difficult for them to know if they have solved it correctly.

You should explain that not all words will work the way they expect. You may want to occasionally work with words that are exceptions (such as *cow - snow, fork - work*). It is also important to validate for children when a word does not work as expected. Sometimes they will make a nonsense word or a word that should follow a spelling pattern you are working with, but doesn't. (For example, when a child changes *my* to *hy*, the teacher says, "You are right, it could be spelled like that, but this time we spell it like this: *high*." Or, if a child changes *like* to *rike*, the teacher says, "Yes, if that was a real word, that is how we might spell it."

Transferring into Reading

Again, the goal of using the magnetic letters is to teach children to independently problem solve new words in text. After observing that students are understanding and seeing parts in words with the magnetic letters, the teacher needs to quickly support the transfer of this strategy into text reading.

Example 1: Most Support

Jed stops on the word *call*.

Teacher: Do you see something you know that might help you? [The teacher uses a masking card, or her finger, to cover the letter *c*.]

The teacher is prompting Jed to notice how this new word looks like a word he knows. She then shows him the part to attend to.

Example 2: Less Support

Maria stops on the word *shout*.

Teacher: Where would you break that word?
           or
           Do you see something you know that might help?
           Put your finger there and break the word apart.

When the teacher asks, "Where would you break that word?" she is actually asking Maria to ask that of herself. The teacher directs Maria to cover part of the word and find something she knows. Maria will learn from these specific directions how to do this by herself next time.

Example 3: Minimal Support

Matt stops on the word *stand*.

Teacher: What could you try?
           or
           What are you going to do to help yourself?

This is a much more general call for action by the teacher. Matt should then ask himself, "Do I know a word like that?" or "Where could I take this word apart?" If he needs more help to see if it is like something he knows, he may cover up part of the word.

Teachers will find many opportunities to support children to problem solve new words. It is important to remember that problem solving using visual information is not always the quickest and most efficient way to solve unknown words. Teachers need to prompt children to use all sources of information. What follows here is an example of what this might look like to a child. Nick attempts to read a new book with his teacher's help (Figures 4–9 and 4–10).

The teacher is prompting Nick to use all sources of information. Sometimes in a teacher's zest for teaching students to use visual information, prompting for the use of meaning or structure is forgotten. While Nick could have used visual information to solve both *boots* and *sled*, it was much easier and more efficient for him to use meaning to solve those unknown words.

The teacher plays a critical role in helping the novice reader learn to problem solve new words independently. Fountas and Pinnell (1996) tell us, "When readers learn how words and word parts work,

Nick's reading of *The Big Snow*

From *The Big Snow*

-       ✓   ✓
It   had   snowed.   *The teacher writes* it *on a white*
                                            board.
                                            T: This is the same word, only
                                               with an uppercase I.
                                            N: It!

    ✓   ✓   ✓   ✓   ✓   ✓
Zack   put on   his coat and

✓   ✓   ✓   ✓   -
his hat   and   his   boots.   T: Try that again and think
                                      what would make sense.
✓   ✓   -
He went outside   T: Do you see something that
                                      might help you?
                                      Nick doesn't respond. T *covers up*
✓   ✓   ✓   ✓   ✓   side *making only* out *visible.*
to play in the snow.   N: Out!   Outsssside

Figure 4–9 Nick's reading of The Big Snow

Page 4

✓   -   ✓   ✓
Zack got his sled.

T: Do you know a word like
   that? *She covers up the g.*
N: *not!*
T: Yes, so the new word is . . .
   She shows the g again.
N: *got!*

✓   ✓   ✓   ✓   ✓
He went down the hill

✓   ✓   -
on his sled.

T: Check the picture. It will
   help you.
N: Oh! *Sled!*

✓   ✓   ✓   ✓   ✓
"Mom, come and see me!

✓ ✓ go-ing ✓ ✓   ✓   ✓
I am going down the hill!"

T: I like how you saw the two
   parts in *going* to help yourself!
   *go-ing! She shows two parts
   with a masking card.*

✓   ✓
shouted Zack.

Zack got his sled.
He went down the hill on his sled.
"Mom, come and see me!
I am going down the hill!"
shouted Zack.

Figure 4–10 The Big Snow

they use their understanding to 'take apart' new and unfamiliar words. The teacher's goal is to help each reader develop this set of strategies" (168). The teacher must first teach by demonstration and then prompt for the child to use what he or she has been taught.

Opportunities for Independent Practice

Teachers can organize some learning center activities to support children to practice reading and writing new words by analogy and taking words apart.

Word Sorts

The following activity will support children to quickly notice common onsets or rimes and support them to be able to read a new word or write a new word by analogy.

- On three different envelopes, write a word that you have been using as a common sight word and that follows a common spelling pattern. For example, consider the words *look*, *cat*, and *will*.
- For each of these words, come up with four or five new words that start or end the same way. For example, you could use *look*, *book*, *took*, *shook*; *pat*, *hat*, *sat*, *fat*; *bill*, *pill*, *hill*, *drill*. Write the words on index-sized cards.
- For each envelope, make an answer-key card that lists the words that match. Place each answer key in the corresponding envelope.
- Mix the index cards together and place them with the three envelopes in a baggie that seals or a box.

Show the children how to remove the word cards, sort them, and then check with the card in the envelope for correctness. (See Figure 4–11.) Alternatively, you can have the children write down their sorted words on a recording sheet.

For more on word sorts, see *Word Matters* (Fountas and Pinnell 1989) and *Phonics They Use* (Cunningham 1995).

Making New Words

The following activity will support children to write a new word by analogy.

- On an index-sized card, write a word you have used during a teaching session.

Figure 4–11 Children sorting words

- In a small baggie or box, place magnetic letters to make new words. For example, if you have written the word *not* on the card, place the letters *o*, *t*, plus *p*, *l*, *c*, *g*, *r*, and *d* in the bag.
- Show the children how to make the new word with the magnetic letters and then write it on a recording sheet. (See Figure 4–12.)

Word Book
The following activity will support children to write a new word by analogy.

- Staple together four or five small pages.
- On the front page write a word you have been using to teach analogies.
- Show the children how they can write in their word book new words that look and sound like the word on the cover.

Figure 4–12 Child making words with magnetic letters

Word Making
The following activity will support children to practice adding a letter to the front of a word to make a new word.

- Use two large cubes to make dice.
- On one cube write initial letters (e.g., *b, f, s*).
- On the other cube write small words that the initial letters can be added to (e.g., *it, in, old, all, and, an, at*).
- The children roll the dice and on a recording sheet write the new words. (They will need to consider if it makes a real word!)
- A more advanced activity would be to put letter clusters and blends on the first cube. (See Figure 4–13.)

Bingo
The following activity will support children to quickly notice common onsets or rimes and support them to be able to read and write a new word by analogy.

- Make bingo cards with nine squares, and enough markers for all players.
- In each square write a known word you have been using in word study to teach about rime (e.g., *look, will, got,* and *dad*).
- Make cards with words that have similar rimes (e.g., *took, mill, pot,* and *had*). Place them in a baggie.
- Each child takes a bingo card and markers. Students take turns drawing a card from the baggie. If they draw a word that ends like one of the words on their board they place a marker on it. The play continues until someone covers three words in a line. (See Figure 4–14.) Alternatively, play can continue until all squares are covered.

A harder version would be a bingo game with onsets. On the bingo card, place key words you have used for onset teaching (such as *stop, children,* and *she*). Make cards with similar onsets (e.g., *stick, cheese* and *ship*).

Word Breaking
The following activity will support children to learn how to take words apart, searching for known parts that will help solve a new word.

- On a card, write a large word that has several known parts.
- On the back of the card, write the word broken apart. (For a suggested list see Appendix B.)
- Place the card in a baggie with all the magnetic letters needed to make the word on the card.
- The children take out the magnetic letters and make the word. Then they break the word apart.
- Create five or six of these words and place the baggies with letters and cards all in a box together. Children can check their work by turning the cards over. (See Figure 4–15.)

Large-Group Activities

Word of the Day
The following activity will support children to learn how to take words apart, searching for known parts that will help solve the new word.

Figure 4–13 Cubes for making new words

Figure 4–14 Children playing Bingo with high frequency words

Figure 4–15 Children playing word-breaking game

On a magnetic easel or board leave a word for children to practice taking apart and reading. At some point during the day, they can move the magnetic letters and try to solve what the word is. Review at the end of the day as a large group.

Using the Word Wall
The following activities will help children become familiar with words on the word wall and use the word wall to read and write new words. (See Figure 4–16.)

- Tell children you are thinking of a word that looks and sounds like a word on the word wall. Tell them the word and ask someone to locate a word like it on the word wall.
- Show them a word on the word wall and ask them to write a word that looks and sounds like that word. They can do this on a scrap of paper, or on small whiteboards.

Figure 4–16 Dee McWilliams' first-grade word wall

- Make up a rhyme for a word on the word wall and see if they can find the word. For example: My *bed* is _____ (red).
- Make up clues about a word on the word wall and let the children look for it. Later, the children will be able to make up clues for each other.

Using Poems and Chants

The following activity will help children see the visual similarities of words and hear how some words sound alike.

Display a poem or chant in a chart. On a large card hold up a word they all know. Have the children come up and locate words with the same onset or rime on the chart. Use highlighter tape to mark the words.

Rhyming Activities

The following activity will help children see the visual similarities of words and listen for and hear how some words sound alike.

- Display a known word. Ask who can name a word that sounds the same. Toss the volunteer a beanbag. As volunteers catch the beanbag they say the original word and then the new word and toss the beanbag back to the teacher.
- When it is time to line up the class, write a word on the board. Say, "Can you think of a word that almost sounds and looks like this word?" Call on volunteers. If they are correct they can line up. Change the word on the board as they run out of ideas.

Summary

You will start to think of lots of ways you can provide independent practice for using analogy and taking words apart. It is important to remember that you are trying to reinforce how to go from a known word to a new word while reading and writing. The words you use must be words the children know. Don't overwhelm the children with a lot of word families. Avoid starting with unknown word parts.

As you focus on teaching children to be more proficient in their use of visual information, that teaching is most effective in the context of real reading and real writing. The strong reader is always searching for and using a variety of sources of information. We need to foster the child's ability to use all sources of information in an independent way. Careful observation through the use of running records will help you examine how your teaching is going.

Chapter 5

Selecting and Organizing Materials

Once upon a time teaching children about words and letters only required a desk, pencil, and workbook for each child. As our understanding of the learning process has grown, the need for different materials and a new classroom organization has become apparent. Teachers need to provide a variety of learning opportunities to successfully reach all of the children. Because children will need demonstration from the more expert word users, a large-group setting and a small-group instructional setting will be essential. Children also need to explore and practice new understandings with their peers, so a classroom with an independent area for word work is also important.

Large-Group Work

Most teachers organize their classroom with a space to gather the whole class together. It is important that the place for this large-group gathering allows for easy view of a word wall. The teacher will want quick access to an easel that can be used for interactive writing and shared reading. (See Figure 5–1.) Other items the teacher will want to store in the large-gathering area include a pocket chart, a container (such as a basket or bin) for a Magna-doodle or whiteboard and markers, and a box of magnetic letters organized alphabetically.

Figure 5–1 Easel area with materials

Small-Group Work

During small-group work, teachers need to have easy access to various materials. A bookshelf behind the reading table or some bins behind the teacher works well. It is important to have available a magnetic easel. This can be either a large easel that stands on its own near the table or circle, or a small easel that sits on top of the table. The teacher should have a large container of magnetic letters, with multiples of all letters. A whiteboard for the teacher and small whiteboards for each child in the group are very useful. (See Figure 5–2.)

Independent Work

During independent work, the children must have easy access to materials. A bookshelf with bins and containers works well. If there is enough space, place a small table nearby to keep the learning center activities and directions ready for students. If there isn't a table or enough space, children can get materials from the center and take them to their table or desk. The learning center activities can be organized easily and inexpensively with small sealable baggies, boxes, muffin tins, and plastic containers. It is helpful to

Figure 5–2 Small-group teaching area

label containers and boxes so that you and the children can find letters easily and return them to the right place. (See Figure 5–3.)

Here is a list of materials you may want at the independent alphabet center. (See Appendix C for ordering information.)

- Three slotted boxes for magnetic letters
- Three or four sets of uppercase plastic magnetic letters
  (stored in one box)
- Five or more sets of lowercase plastic magnetic letters
  (stored in one box)
- Five sets of foam magnetic letters (stored in one box)
- Four sets of link letters, which link together to form words
- Tactile letters for tracing (such as made of sandpaper)
- Alphabet letter books
- Pointers
- Pocket chart
- Six small whiteboards, markers, and erasers

Figure 5–3 Alphabet center

- Small chalkboard, chalk, and erasers
- Index cards for making word cards
- Alphabet cards, puzzles, sound games, and so forth to be used in a variety of ways
- Magnetic board
- Plastic containers, sealable plastic baggies, muffin tins, and small boxes for storing and sorting activities
- Sand or salt tray (Figure 5–4)

Selecting Magnetic Letters
There are many styles of magnetic letters on the market. It is important to have a variety of letters so children become flexible with letter shapes. You may want to have some letters with curves and tails

Figure 5–4 Sand tray

and some straight-edged letters. The less expensive letters often slip around on the board. Quercetti magnetic letters, made in Italy, are recommended. Purchase both straight-tailed letter sets and D'Neallian letter sets. The magnets are strong and stick well to the board. Link letter, letters which link together to make words, are also a nice resource for the alphabet center (Figure 5–5).

New to the market are foam magnetic letters. You probably want to keep these in a separate container from plastic magnetic letters. Appendix C lists distributors of magnetic letters and other letter resources.

Organizing Magnetic Letters

It is easy to organize magnetic letters for easy access. A large cookie sheet can be used. Pile letters alphabetically on the sheet. Letters can also be easily organized in a plastic container with slots. The distributors of letters sell containers for this purpose (see Appendix C), but you can also pick up an inexpensive plastic fishing tackle box in the sporting section of a discount store (Figure 5–6).

Figure 5–5 Child making a word with link letters

Conclusion

Once a classroom is set up and organized, teachers will discover just how much children enjoy exploring letters and words. Some children see word parts, make connections to their reading and writing, and seem to learn effortlessly. For other children, learning how words work takes time, practice, and most important, clear instruction from a teacher.

Some children who really struggle may need an early intervention. Reading Recovery teachers work one-on-one with children who are most at risk of failing to learn to read. As part of their daily lessons with these children, Reading Recovery teachers help children learn about words and letters. These lessons are designed for the individual needs of the learner. Because the lessons are designed for the individual child, the child's learning rate is accelerated, helping the child catch up with peers.

Most children do not need an intervention. (In a typical classroom, only about 20 percent of the children need Reading Recovery.) Most children, however, do need some form of instruction to learn

Figure 5–6 Storage box for magnetic letters

about how print works. When teachers plan lessons and follow-up activities, it is very important to keep in mind the ultimate goal: fostering proficient, independent readers and writers. The goal is never the finished activity itself! There can be no precanned sequence of lessons, because for each child or group of children the path will be different. Assessment is needed to establish where the children are starting, and ongoing assessment is needed to help teachers gather information on what has been learned and what remains to be learned. From this information, teachers can design effective large-group, small-group, and independent learning activities.

Appendix A: Finding Word Analogies

The list of known words contains words children commonly learn first. Teachers should generally begin with the *known word*. Therefore, if the children learn a different word first, begin there. For example, if children learn the word *way* before the word *day*, use *way* as the word to change.

Group 1

Known Word	Easier New Words	More Difficult New Words
look	hook, took, cook, book	shook, crook, brook
day	way, hay, lay, pay	stay, gray, play
got	not, pot, hot, rot	spot, knot, shot
will	hill, fill, pill, Bill, mill, dill	grill, still, chill
my	by	shy, why, fry, pry
cat	rat, fat, hat, mat, sat, bat, pat	brat, chat, flat, that
make	take, cake, lake, rake	shake, flake, snake, brake
dad	had, sad, bad, mad	glad, clad
like	bike, Mike, hike, pike	spike, strike

Known Word	Easier New Words	More Difficult New Words
can	fan, van, pan, tan, man, ran	plan, clan, Stan, than, bran
me	be, he, we	she
see	bee, wee, tee	tree, knee, free, three
no	so, go	pro

Group 2

Known Word	Easier New Words	More Difficult New Words
came	name, same, lame, tame, game	shame, blame, flame, frame
cap	nap, lap, gap, rap, zap	strap, trap, chap, flap, scrap
gave	cave, wave, save, rave	grave, brave, slave, shave
dear	fear, hear, near, rear, year	clear, shear, smear, spear
red	bed, led, fed, wed, Ted	fled, sled, shed, sped
keep	beep, weep, jeep, deep	cheep, sheep, sleep, sweep
feet	meet, beet	greet, sleet, street, sweet, tweet
well	sell, tell, bell, fell, yell	shell, smell, spell, swell
get	jet, wet, met, yet, let, set, bet	fret
could	would	should
sun	run, gun, fun, bun, pun	stun, shun
down	town, gown	drown, crown, clown, brown
now	wow, how, bow, cow	chow, plow, brow

Appendix B:
Taking Words Apart

Word	Easier Words for Breaking	More Difficult Words for Breaking
in	pin, win, sin, fin, bin	chin, grin, shin, thinner, winning, winter, dinner
at	cat, sat, mat, bat, rat, pat	chat, drat, chatter, flatter, patting, catcher, patch, match, Saturday
it	hit, pit, sit, bit, lit, fit	grit, flit, quit, glitter, hitter, sitting, stitch, pitcher, critter, ditch, witch
and	band, sand, land, hand	stand, grand, bland, sandy, landed, sandwich, sandal, handle, Grandma
am	ham, Sam, ram, Pam, yam	slam, cram, sham, clam, lamp, stamp, tramp, hammer, lamb

Word	Easier Words for Breaking	More Difficult Words for Breaking
all	ball, call, tall, mall, wall, fall, hall	stall, calling, small, squall, caller, taller, smaller
out	lout, pout, gout, bout	scout, shout, spout, sprout, trout, about, shouting
up	pup, cup, sup	supper, puppy
us	bus, pus	plus, just, must, trust, crust, thrust, rusting
or	for	fort, fork, porter, before, torn, pork, morning, short, stork, corn, corner
ox	box, fox, lox	boxer, foxing
ate	gate, hate, late, date, fate	crate, plate, skate, state, later, crater

Appendix C:
List of Suppliers

You can obtain magnetic letters, link letters, whiteboards, and alphabet cards from the following suppliers:

Resources for Reading
P.O. Box 5783
Redwood City, CA 94063
Phone: 800-278-7323
Fax: 650-747-0141

Michael Associates
409 Beatty Road, Suite 100
Monroeville, PA 15146
Phone: 800-869-1467
Fax: 412-374-9363

Steps to Literacy
P.O. Box 6263
Bridgewater, NJ 08807
Phone: 800-895-2804
Fax: 732-560-8699

You can obtain alphabet books from one of the following book distributors:

(Dominie Letter books)
Dominie Press, Inc.
1949 Kellogg Avenue
Carlsbad, CA 92008
Phone: 760-431-8000
Fax: 760-431-8777

(PM Alphabet Starters)
Rigby
P.O. Box 797
Crystal Lake, IL 60039-0797
Phone: 800-822-8661
Fax: 800-427-4429

Appendix D: Titles of Leveled Books

Early Emergent 1

Title	Series	Publisher
A *Yummy Lunch*	Early Emergent 4	Pioneer Valley Educ. Press
At *School*	Sunshine	Wright Group
Dad	PM Starters 1	Rigby
The *Fox*	Emergent Set	Richard C. Owens
The *Go-carts*	PM Starters 1	Rigby
I *Can Fly*	Sunshine	Wright Group
I *Like*	Sunshine	Wright Group
I *Like Balloons*	Reading Corners	Dominie Press
I *Like to Eat*	Reading Corners	Dominie Press
I *Read*	Reading Corners	Dominie Press
Look	Sunshine	Wright Group
Me	PM Starters 1	Rigby
Mom	PM Starters 1	Rigby
Moms	Handprints B	Educator Publishing Service

Title	Series	Publisher
Pets	PM Starters 1	Rigby
Playground Fun	Handprints B	Educator Publishing Service
Playing	PM Starters 1	Rigby
The Shopping Mall	PM Starters 1	Rigby
The Skier	PM Starters 1	Rigby
The Traffic Jam	Handprints B	Educator Publishing Service
Too Fast	Reading Corners	Dominie Press
Where is Gabby?	Early Emergent 4	Pioneer Valley Educ. Press

Early Emergent 2

Title	Series	Publisher
At the Ocean	Early Emergent 3	Pioneer Valley Educ. Press
Baby Animals	Reading Corners	Dominie Press
Balloons	Early Emergent 2	Pioneer Valley Educ. Press
A Birthday Party	Early Emergent 1	Pioneer Valley Educ. Press
Fruit Salad	Early Emergent 1	Pioneer Valley Educ. Press
Fun on the Slide	Early Emergent 3	Pioneer Valley Educ. Press
Gabby Visits Buster	Early Emergent 3	Pioneer Valley Educ. Press
The Ghost	Storybox	Wright Group
Going Up and Down	Early Emergent 1	Pioneer Valley Educ. Press
Hard at Work	Early Emergent 2	Pioneer Valley Educ. Press
Here's Skipper		Seedlings
I Can Read	Sunshine	Wright Group

Title	Series	Publisher
I Love Camping	Early Emergent 2	Pioneer Valley Educ. Press
Ice Cream	Ready to Read	Pacific Learning
Jump Frog	Sunshine	Wright Group Seedlings
Making a Bird	PM Plus	Wright Group
The Merry-go-round	Sunshine	Rigby
My Busy Day	Early Emergent 4	Pioneer Valley Educ. Press
My Family	Sunshine	Wright Group
My Home	Sunshine	Wright Group
My Picture	Carousel Readers	Dominie Press
My Puppy	Storybox	Wright Group
The Pencil	PM Starters 2	Rigby
Playing with My Cat	Early Emergent 3	Pioneer Valley Educ. Press
Plop	Storybox	Wright Group
Runaway Monkey		Seedlings
The Way I Go to School	PM Starters 1	Rigby
What Am I?	Handprints B	Educators Publishing Service
Where Can I Write?	Early Emergent 3	Pioneer Valley Educ. Press

Early Emergent 3

Title	Series	Publisher
At the Zoo	DC Little Readers	Houghton Mifflin
Baby Wakes Up	PM Plus	Rigby
Blocks	Early Emergent 1	Pioneer Valley Educ. Press
Come and Play Cat	Early Emergent 4	Pioneer Valley Educ. Press
Copycat	Storybox	Wright Group
Farm Chores	Early Emergent 4	Pioneer Valley Educ. Press
Fun with Mo and Toots	Ready to Read	Pacific Learning
Going for a Ride	Early Emergent 1	Pioneer Valley Educ. Press

Title	Series	Publisher
Jack and Billy	PM Plus	Rigby
The Lazy Pig	PM Storybooks	Rigby
The Little Red Hen	Windmill	Wright Group
The Merry-go-round	PM Storybooks	Rigby
My Dog	Early Emergent 1	Pioneer Valley Educ. Press
My Lunch	Early Emergent 1	Pioneer Valley Educ. Press
Old Tuatara	Ready to Read	Pacific Learning
The Photo Book	PM Storybooks	Rigby
Photo Time	PM Plus	Pioneer Valley Educ. Press
Playing in the Snow	Early Emergent 1	Rigby
Sam and Bingo	PM Plus	Rigby
Sam's Balloon	PM Plus	Rigby
Splashing Dad	Early Emergent 1	Pioneer Valley Educ. Press
Tiger, Tiger	PM Storybooks	Rigby
Wake Up, Dad	PM Storybooks	Rigby

Appendix E:
Book Publishers

Dominie Press, Inc.
1949 Kellogg Avenue
Carlsbad, CA 92008
Phone: 760-431-8000
Fax: 760-431-8777
www.dominie.com

Educators Publishing Service, Inc.
31 Smith Place Dept. NS
Cambridge, MA 02138-1089
Phone: 800-225-5750
Fax: 617-547-0412
www.epsbooks.com

Pacific Learning
15342 Graham Street
Huntington Beach, CA 92649-0723
Phone: 800-279-0737
Fax: 714-895-5087
www.pacificlearning.com

Pioneer Valley Educational Press
P.O. Box 9375
North Amherst, MA 01059-9375
Phone: 413-548-3906
Fax: 413-548-4914
www.pvep.com

Rigby
P.O. Box 797
Crystal Lake, IL 60039-0797
Phone: 800-822-8661
Fax: 800-427-4429
www.rigby.com

Seedling Publications, Inc.
4522 Indianola Avenue
Columbus, OH 43214-2246
Phone: 877-857-SEED
Fax: 614-267-4205
www.seedlingpub.com

The Wright Group
19201 120th Avenue NE
Bothell, WA 98011-9512
Phone: 800-648-2970
Fax: 800-543-7323
www.WrightGroup.com

Appendix F: Prompts for Problem Solving with Visual Information

High Level of Teacher Support

- Make the word with magnetic letters and help the child break the word apart. Ask, "Can you see some parts of this word that will help you?"

- Write a known word (that looks like the unknown word) on a whiteboard and write the new word underneath. Say, "This word looks and sounds like a word you know."

- Put your finger over the first letter(s) of the unknown word (showing the part that looks like a known word). Say, "This word ends like a word you know."

- Cover up the end of the word.
  Say, "This word starts like a word you know."

Medium Level of Teacher Support

- When the child comes to an unknown word, ask, "Do you know a word like that?" or "Where could you take that word apart?" or "Do you know a word that starts like that?" or "Do you know a word that ends like that?"

Low Level of Teacher Support

- When the child stops at a new word, ask, "What could you try?" or "What do you think it could be?" or "What do you know that might help?"

Bibliography

Adams, M. 1990. *Beginning to Read: Thinking and Learning About Print.* Cambridge, MA: MIT Press.

Beaver, J., et al. 1997. *Developmental Reading Assessment.* Glenview, IL: Celebration Press.

Calkins, L. M. 1986. *The Art of Teaching Writing.* Portsmouth, NH: Heinemann.

Clay, M. M. 1991. *Becoming Literate: The Construction of Inner Control.* Portsmouth, NH: Heinemann.

———. *An Observation Survey of Early Literacy Achievement.* Portsmouth, NH: Heinemann.

———. *Reading Recovery: A Guidebook for Teachers in Training.* Portsmouth, NH: Heinemann.

———. 2000. *Running Records for Classroom Teachers.* Portsmouth, NH: Heinemann.

———. *Changes Over Time in Children's Literacy Development.* Portsmouth, NH: Heinemann.

Clay, M. M., M. Gill, T. Glynn, T. McNaughton, and K. Salmon. 1993. *Record of Oral Language and Biks and Gutches.* Auckland, New Zealand: Heinemann.

Cunningham, P. M. 1995. *Phonics They Use.* New York: HarperCollins College Publishers.

Dorn, L., C. French, and T. Jones. 1998. *Apprenticeship in Literacy*. York, ME: Stenhouse Publishers.

Fisher, B, and E. F. Medvic. 2000. *Perspectives on Shared Reading: Planning and Practice*. Portsmouth, NH: Heinemann.

Fountas, I. C., and G. S. Pinnell. 1989. *Word Matters*. Portsmouth, NH: Heinemann.

——— . 1996. *Guided Reading: Good First Teaching for All Children*. Portsmouth, NH: Heinemann.

Goswami, U., and P. Bryant. 1990. *Phonological Skills and Learning to Read*. Hillsdale, NJ: Lawrence Erlbaum.

Lyons, C. A. 1999. "Letter Learning in the Early Literacy Classroom." In *Voices on Word Matters*, edited by I. C. Fountas and G. S. Pinnell, pp. 57–66. Portsmouth, NH: Heinemann.

Malcolm, M. 1983. *I Can Read*. Wellington, New Zealand: (Ready to Read) School Publications.

McCarrier, A., and I. Patacca. 1999. "Kindergarten Explorations of Letter, Sounds, and Words." In *Voices on Word Matters*, edited by I. C. Fountas and G. S. Pinnell, pp. 45–56. Portsmouth, NH: Heinemann.

McCarrier, A., G. S. Pinnell, and I. C. Fountas. 2000. *Interactive Writing: How Language and Literacy Come Together, K–2*. Portsmouth, NH: Heinemann.

Opitz, M. 2000. *Rhymes and Reasons: Literature and Language Play for Phonological Awareness*. Portsmouth, NH: Heinemann.

Pinnell, G. S. 2000. *Reading Recovery: An Analysis of a Research-Based Reading Intervention*. Columbus, OH: Reading Recovery Council of North America.

Pinnell, G. S., and I. C. Fountas. 1998. *Word Matters: Teaching Phonics and Spelling in the Reading/Writing Classroom*. Portsmouth, NH: Heinemann.

Pinnell, G. S., and I. C. Fountas, ed. 1999. *Voices on Word Matters*. Portsmouth, NH: Heinemann.

Randell, B., J. Giles, and A. Smith. 1996. *Mom*. Crystal Lake, IL: Rigby.